PENGUIN BOOKS

A PARLIAMENT

of

OWLS

D1157915

A PARLIAMENT

of

OWLS

PENGUIN BOOKS

an armoury of aardvarks

a gang of alpacas

a weight of albatrosses

a cluster of antelope

an army of ants

a shrewdness of apes

a flange of baboons

a colony of badgers

a sleuth of bears

a colony of beavers

a hive of bees

a siege of bitterns

a sounder of boars

a chain of bobolinks

a gang of buffalo

a bellowing of bullfinches

a drove of bullocks

a rabble of butterflies

a wake of buzzards

a flock of camels

a herd of caribou

an army of caterpillars

a clutter of cats

a kine of cattle

a coalition of cheetahs

a brood of chickens

a clutch of chicks

a cartload of chimpanzees

a colony of chinchillas

a flight of cormorants

a pack of coyotes

a bushel of crabs

a siege of cranes

a bask of crocodiles

a murder of crows

a parcel of deer

a pack of dogs

a pod of dolphins

a drove of donkeys

a flight of doves

a raft of ducks

a convocation of eagles

a herd of elephants

a gang of elk

a mob of emus

a business of ferrets

a charm of finches

a school of fish

a flamboyance of flamingos

a swarm of flies

a skulk of foxes

a knot of frogs

a gaggle of geese

a horde of gerbils

a tower of giraffes

a cloud of gnats

an implausibility of gnus

a trip of goats

a glint of goldfish

a bloat of hippopotamuses

a parcel of hogs

a nest of hornets

a harras of horses

a pack of hounds

a charm of hummingbirds

a clan of hyenas

a mess of iguanas

a party of jays

a smack of jellyfish

a mob of kangaroos

a kindle of kittens

a deceit of lapwings

an exaltation of larks

a leap of leopards

a pride of lions

a plague of locusts

a congregation of magpies

a mischief of mice

a labour of moles

a troop of monkeys

a herd of moose

a scourge of mosquitoes

a watch of nightingales

a buffoonery of orangutans

a school of orca whales

a pride of ostriches

a bevy of otters

a parliament of owls

a drove of oxen

a bed of oysters

a company of parrots

an ostentation of peacocks

a colony of penguins

a bouquet of pheasants

a flock of pigeons

a drove of pigs

a farrow of piglets

a shoal of pilchards

an impossibility of platypuses

a wing of plovers

a chine of polecats

an improbability of puffins

a prowl of puma

a litter of puppies

a covey of quail

a down of rabbits

a gaze of raccoons

an unkindness of ravens

a crash of rhinoceroses

a run of salmon

a squabble of seagulls

a herd of seahorses

a spring of seals

a school of sharks

a fold of sheep

a walk of snails

a pit of snakes

a host of sparrows

a murmuration of starlings

a drift of swans

a flock of swifts

an acre of terns

a mutation of thrushes

an ambush of tigers

a knot of toads

a rafter of turkeys

a bale of turtles

a nest of vipers

a wake of vultures

a mob of wallabies

a pod of walruses

a sounder of warthogs

a sneak of weasels

a herd of wildebeest

a pack of wolves

a warren of wombats

a descent of woodpeckers

a zeal of zebras

PENGUIN BOOKS

Published by the Penguin Group
Penguin Group (Australia)
250 Camberwell Road, Camberwell, Victoria 3124, Australia
(a division of Pearson Australia Group Pty Ltd)
Penguin Group (USA) Inc.
375 Hudson Street, New York, New York 10014, USA
Penguin Group (Canada)
90 Eglinton Avenue East, Suite 700, Toronto ON M4P 2Y3, Canada
(a division of Pearson Penguin Canada Inc.)
Penguin Books Ltd
80 Strand, London WC2R 0RL, England
Penguin Ireland
25 St Stephen's Green, Dublin 2, Ireland
(a division of Penguin Books Ltd)
Penguin Books India Pvt Ltd
11 Community Centre, Panchsheel Park,
New Delhi – 110 017, India
Penguin Group (NZ)
Cnr Airborne and Rosedale Roads, Albany, Auckland,
New Zealand
(a division of Pearson New Zealand Ltd)
Penguin Books (South Africa) (Pty) Ltd
24 Sturdee Avenue, Rosebank, Johannesburg 2196,
South Africa

Penguin Books Ltd, Registered Offices: 80 Strand, London, WC2R 0RL, England

First published by Penguin Group (Australia), a division of Pearson Australia Group Pty Ltd, 2005

1 3 5 7 9 10 8 6 4 2

Design by Claire Tice © Penguin Group (Australia)
Cover photograph © Getty Images
Printed in China by Everbest Printing Co. Ltd

National Library of Australia
Cataloguing-in-Publication data:

A Parliament of Owls.

1. Animals – Pictorial works.
2. English language – Collective nouns.

ISBN 0 143 00433 6

591

www.penguin.com.au